Behind the Mask

Felecia Ann Carter

Felecia Ann Carter

Copyright @2021

DEDICATION

This book is dedicated in memory of my lost loved ones: my parents L.E. and Betty Lee Carter, my sister Celestine Carter White, my brother Sargent Sharron Andre's Carter, my nephew Donovan Lewis, my Maternal Grandparents Rosa Lee and Willie Amacker, my paternal grandparents Estella and Henderson Carter, and all my uncles, aunts, and cousins.

Acknowledgements

First, I want to thank God, who is the head of my life. My Daughter Quinlyn, who is the love of my life, thank you for loving me. Rondrea Nash who is my second daughter, she has always been my baby. Special thanks to my sister Cynthia, without her I wouldn't be here today; I love you baby girl. My sisters Gloria, Shirley, Brenda, Renee, and Gale, thanks for just loving me. My brother L.E. Jr, the Lord has brought us a mighty long way. I love you. To my pastor/nephew/brother Micah, thanks for praying for me and not giving up on me. Love you Evangelist LaTunga McCray for encouraging me to tell my story even though it made me totally transparent. Love you Evangelist Angela Newton for reconnecting with me just when I needed it the most. To my sister since first grade Shirley Patterson Brunson, friends/sisters for life. Brandi, I have not forgotten you my encourager, and listening ear, I am forever grateful to you, love you girl. All my nieces and nephews, I love you guys.

Tabatha Lewis-Byrd, thanks for the listening ear and directing me to the right person. Lastly, special thanks to Dr Tomekia Luckett for all her help coaching me on the steps I needed to take to write this book. I will forever be grateful.

Contents

Chapter 1

***

The Beginning

Growing up in a small rural area of Mississippi called Magnolia, I had the greatest childhood anyone could imagine. Being born the ninth child of eleven to L.E and Betty Amacker Carter two of the greatest parents who ever lived. I was beyond blessed. I was raised in a strict but loving home. My dad was an Elder and later became a Superintendent in the Grand Ole Church of God in Christ. He was a hardworking man, proud but humble; he would work at what was then the Fernwood Industry as a fork lift operator. He always said he could make that forklift do anything. Even though he only had a ninth-grade education, he made sure each of his children were given the opportunity to go to college. He wanted us to have a good education so that we would not have to work hard as he did for a small amount of money.

My daddy wanted us to accomplish things out of life that were not afforded to him in his youth. From his hard work and dedication, he was able to witness seven of his daughters, Gloria, Shirley, Brenda, Renee, Gale, myself and Cynthia become nurses. Four are RNs and three are LPNs, and his baby boy Sharron became a Medic in the United States National Guard reserve. My sister Celestine was the only one who did not go to college for nursing; she majored in office management and was a very hard worker. My oldest brother was a US Army veteran and hardworking factory worker. Also, two of his grandchildren whom he helped to raise, Brandi and Micah, are LPNs.

My daddy loved his family. He would work all day then come home and farm at night to make sure his family had what they needed and some of their wants. After he would work in the fields, he would get dressed and drive as far as Natchez, MS to preach and spread the Gospel of Jesus Christ. He was a powerful and anointed preacher who was highly respected and true to his calling. Daddy was a big and tall man, but he had a real gentle spirit. He was always asking for a kiss—sugar, as he would call it—and a hug. He called me Momo Lisa when I was younger, and would ask me how much I loved him, a little or a lot. It would always be a lot. In my opinion, my daddy was the greatest father who ever lived.

My mother, wow, where do I begin? She was my heart. My mother worked outside the home when we were younger. Every Friday she would bring us a special treat. Most of the time, the treat was a box of Cheez-it crackers that made us feel so special. She would sew some of our clothes, so we always had something nice to wear. I remember when my sister Cynthia and I were baptized; it was during the times when they baptized in the river down the road from Mary's Chapel C.O.G.I.C., a church my dad pastored. My mom made us matching maxi dresses to be baptized. We thought we were princesses in those dresses, they were so beautiful. She made sure we had hot meals every day. When she did not cook or worked late, she taught my older sibling how to cook and take care of the younger kids. When she cooked, she was always the last to eat, making sure her children and husband ate first. I would often see her eating what was left on a saucer. Mama wasn't the type of person that said "I love you" daily, but she showed us in the best way possible by how she cared for us. She was a quiet person, but she had a beautiful smile that would just melt your heart. My mama was genuine. She was my Queen, a sassy dresser; nobody could wear a church hat like my mama. My mama was the greatest mother that ever lived.

I was blessed to be raised in a loving two-parent household, to parents who loved the Lord first and their children next. At a young age they taught us children to stick together and always be there for one another. We all felt special and loved, and we were well taken care of physically. We were also taught that beyond the physical, there was a spiritual side that had to be nurtured. My oldest sister Gloria also played a major part in our care when we were young. She was like our second mom. We were taken to church, not sent to church, on Sundays. Unlike children today, we didn't have a choice; you were going to church, and you could not have your parents late. I didn't understand then, but I do now, and I thank God for my upbringing. We were taught to respect our elders and to say "yes ma'am" and "no sir." We were not allowed to listen or interrupt grown people when they were having a conversation. Our parents raised us; we did not raise ourselves. We were not allowed to wear just anything and hang around just anybody. We never thought we were better than others, but my parents knew hanging around the wrong crowd could get us in some serious trouble.

What happened to parents raising their children? In today's society parents want to be their children's friend and buddy. There is nothing wrong with being your child's friend, as long as you let them know you are the parent and there are boundaries that they are not allowed to cross. When I was growing up, hanging out in clubs and dancing and partying with your parents was out of the question. The only place you were hanging out together was the church house, and the only dance you were doing were the holy ones. Playing cards was out of the question unless you played them when you were left at home alone, but that was a rare occasion.

Strict but loving, my parents had a way of chastising you that hurt your feelings. It hurt your feelings more than it did physically, because you didn't want them to be mad at you. Daddy was the disciplinarian when we got in trouble. Mama would always say, "You going to get a whipping when your daddy gets home." We knew we were in trouble then. We had a closet that was full of old clothes; having so many children, we wore hand me downs from one another. By the time my daddy would make it home, we would have so many layers of clothes on that we wouldn't feel the pain. I don't know why we wasted all that time putting on clothes that we already knew daddy was going to make us pull them off before he started whipping us.

The three musketeers: Cynthia, Sharron, and myself. The three youngest of the bunch, and the three baddest ones as I reflect back. We were always together and always getting in trouble. I remember one time we were playing volleyball on top of the house. We found ways to enjoy ourselves. We didn't have a volleyball net, so we used the roof of the house because it had a slant to it, so the ball would roll back down perfectly when you hit it. One day we were playing volleyball on top of the house Mama was in the kitchen cooking she yelled out, "Y'all better quit hitting that ball on top of that house before y'all break one of these windows." The three musketeers did not listen; we continued to hit that ball like we were professional volleyball players on top of that house until one of us hit the ball and it went straight through the kitchen window, by the stove where Mama was cooking. It's still unclear even to today which one us had actually hit the winning window shot, because we all blamed the other one. But that was the least of our worries when mama hollered,

"Y'all wait until your daddy arrives home." We all took off running trying to get to that treasure chest full of clothes to layer ourselves in, in anticipation of what was next to come. Of course, it didn't work as usual; we were made to strip down to one set. We were not like kids of today, we had no electronic devices to play with, we had no cellphones—we had one rotary dial phone with an extra-long cord that was the only way you were able to walk around and talk from room to room a cordless what not in those days—no Playstation, Nintendo boxes. All you had was jacks, a jump rope, a hula hoop, a ball of some type, and the great outdoors. Oh, how I missed those days of Mama yelling out, "Y'all better quit going in and out this house; stay in or stay out before y'all tear up my screen door." My childhood was great, but soon it was time to grow up and face the realities of life.

Chapter 2

***

Why did I have to grow up?

One thing about Mama and Daddy: you were going to school, you were going to do your homework, and you were going to bring home a good report card. Even though my dad did not know how to read or write, he always insisted on us bring home good grades. My oldest sister Gloria would teach him in the evening time, and he became fluent in reading and writing. I was a good student in school. I made good grades and was well behaved. In my home, misbehaving at school was unacceptable. "Showing out at school" is what we called it. You were going to act like somebody, respect your teacher, and stay out of trouble.

My high school days were fun, but they couldn't last forever. I went straight from high school graduation and started college at Southwest Mississippi Junior College, taking prerequisites for nursing. I wanted to follow in my oldest sister's footsteps and become a nurse. I took my first year of prerequisites and applied for the RN program. But in that day and time, it was hard for a black person to get into the RN program. They were only allowed a certain number each year so I did not get accepted. I applied for the LPN program and was accepted into the next class. The Licensed

Practical Nursing (LPN) program was a twelve-month course from August to August. I did not have a car of my own; as a matter of fact, I couldn't even drive. Daddy would drop me off at school before he went to work, and Mama would pick me up, or I would ride some time with my friend Patricia Gordon Cunnigen. That was my routine for the year until I graduated.

My first job after nursing school was at Southwest Extended Care in McComb, MS and it was a good job. I also worked when needed at Beecham Memorial Hospital in Magnolia. Back then they had a small emergency room that was fun and exciting to work in. Working at Southwest Extended Care was a nursing position I enjoyed as well. I loved talking to the patients and taking care of them on a daily basis. But I left there and went full time at Beacham, because you grow so attached to the patients in the nursing home, and when they start dying it takes a toll on you. This was my first sign that I could not handle death well. I worked at Beacham for a year, then I got a job at what was then called East Louisiana State Hospital in Jackson, LA. This was a mental institution, and I was following in my sister Gloria's footsteps once again, as she was already working there.

Chapter 3

***

What's Love Got to do with it?

Working at East, as we called it, was an interesting job! You encountered all types of patients, with issues such as schizophrenia (a disorder that affect a person's ability to think, feel and behave normally,) bipolar disorder (also called manic depression, a disorder that causes mood swings that range from depressive lows to manic highs,) and clinical depression (also known as major depression, a disorder that characterized by persistently depressed mood that causes loss of interest in daily activities of life.) We also took care of patients who lied about having a particular disorder to avoid jail time. We had patients that were committed by their families because they were a danger to themselves. I heard some gruesome stories at times, but I heard some heartwarming stories as well. It was a wide group of people: African-American, White, Mexican, and Chinese. Mental illness does not discriminate; it affects all races, genders and ages.

I met and became friends with a lot of good people; a couple in particular whom I was extremely close to were my friend Chandra and her entire family, Vinnie, Josephine, Mrs. Neff, Rebecca, and Jackie. We worked closely together and developed a bond that will withstand time. We can go years without talking and seeing each other but when we do reconnect it is just like old times. This is where I met my husband Clyde, when he was a mental health tech. He was tall, dark, and handsome, and stole my heart right away. He was sweet, gentle, and loving. I was so love struck that I didn't realize at the time that we were not on the same level in maturity. I had lived a sheltered life. My dating before this consisted of double dating with one of my sisters at the house. We could not leave L.E. and Betty Carter's house with boys. Daddy would walk backward and forward looking in the living room door by nine o'clock. He would start knocking because it was his bedtime, and time for them to hit the road.

Clyde was used to partying with friends and having a good time. I was in the church, saved and filled with the Holy Ghost, and he would not enter the church doors. We were unequally yoked, as the scripture says, but I was in love. I was on my own for the first time. I had my own house; I was renting between Clinton and Jackson, LA, about fifteen minutes from the job. Mama and Daddy helped me move; they brought my furniture out of my room at their house to my house in Clinton. My mama didn't like to ride long distances, but she did it for me. She helped me unload and unpack everything. Then she would call me every day; she had my number memorized.

I had my own car, my own house, making my own money. I was a full-grown adult, not knowing that in the future I would wish I was a child again. Clyde and I started dating. We kept it a secret at the beginning because we worked at the same hospital. I was a nurse, and he was a certified nursing assistant (CNA). We didn't have a problem with each other's job position, but we knew it was going to be the talk of the hospital. We would meet in the mornings and go hang out in Baton Rouge, LA until close to time to go to work. We both worked the 3-11 shift, then we would head home to get ready for work. We worked on different buildings at the hospital, but sometimes he would get pulled or I would get pulled, and we would end up working the same building. Those were the good days.

We continued to date and get to know each other. I had my own place, and he was living in his grandmother's house next door to his mother Mary. We continued this living arrangement for a while, but as we grew closer, he gradually started moving his things into my house. And I let it happen; even though I knew it was not right, I was in love. At the time I was heavily involved in the church, I was saved and sanctified, Holy Ghost filled and fire baptized. Yes, sometimes we do slip and come short of the Glory of God, because we are flesh and we are human. Before long he had completely moved in and had his own space in the closet and his toothbrush was in the bathroom. I was officially "shacking," as the old people would say. We lived like this for a while, but I was never comfortable with it. Number one, I was not honoring my vow to God to live a holy and sanctified life. I knew I wasn't living a holy life, because 1 Corinthians 7:9 says it's better to marry then burn and we were two unmarried people living together in sin. Number two, I knew Mama knew I was shacking, because you couldn't fool or keep anything hidden from her; she always just knew. She had this look and special nod of her head that let you know she already knew what was going on.

After a while I got tired of feeling uncomfortable in my own house. I told Clyde we were going to have to get married if we are going to live together, and he said let's do it. This one was one of the biggest decisions of my life, and one of my biggest mistakes. Proverbs 28:25 states that making hasty and rash decisions is not good, as it means you don't trust God. We thought we were doing the right thing. We had the Minister for the patients at the hospital to give us marriage counseling. Sometimes we think we are fixing the situation, but we are only making it worse.

We decided to have a small wedding at my sister Gloria and her husband at the time Carl's house in Clinton. We could not afford a big wedding; I was basically paying all the bills for the both of us, because most of his check went to child support for his daughter Jamie that he had fathered in a previous relationship. I didn't mind because I was in "Love."

1 Peter 4:8 says love hides a multitude of faults, and that's true. We were so in love, all of the flaws were overlooked. And I am a real woman; I did not talk to him negatively one time about him paying child support, because that was his duty as a father. The child did not ask to be born, and it was his responsibility. I would have expected the same thing if I was ordered to receive child support for my child, but when it was my time to receive child support, well that's a whole different story.

We got married, and I wore a borrowed white dress from Mama because I couldn't afford one of my own. Clyde was dressed in black slacks and a nice vest that was really too big for him, but it was the only thing we could find at such a short notice. Mama and Daddy came, even though Mama did not want me to get married. She came and supported me, and my daddy performed the ceremony. Young ladies, take my advice: listen to your mother when she says don't get married to a person, it's something that she sees that's way beyond our understanding. Wisdom is priceless.

The wedding ceremony was finally over, and my daddy had just married his daughter off to Clyde Sambo—or as my daddy called him, Clyde Gumbo. My daddy makes me want to shake my head sometimes, but I couldn't help but love him. Carl took off work to cook for us, and he had cooked so much food. Clyde then proceeded to pop the trunk of the car and started pulling out the alcoholic beverages from the cooler. I was so ashamed, because my Daddy and Mama was there. Daddy probably didn't notice it, but Betty Lee Amacker Carter didn't miss a thing.

Once the wedding was over, we settled into married life. I would go to Mississippi every first and third Sunday, because that was our scheduled church Sundays at the time. But I was always alone, because he continued to not attend church with me. I have always wanted someone that would attend church with me. I always loved to see husbands and wives in church together, and girlfriend and boyfriend attending church together. This never happened for me; maybe the next go around, if the God's willing and the creek do not rise.

Chapter 4

***

The Enjoyment of Motherhood

The marriage was going okay at this time. Clyde had left East and had started driving trucks cross-country. Even though he had a better job making more money, he was taken back to court for an increase in child support by his daughter's mother because of his higher pay. The increase in child support kept us in the same boat we were in: struggling, with me working at the hospital and doing Home Health in the mornings before work. When Clyde came in off the road, all he wanted to do was catch up and party with his friends. This went on until I found out I was carrying the love of my life. I was going to be a mother. I had always babysat my nieces and nephews and helped take care of them. I was finally having a child of my own.

Clyde took a job driving locally, so that meant even less income and more stress on me. I think that's when my battle with depression began. He was bringing in less money, and since he was home every day now that meant even more partying with his friends. Some nights I would stay up all night worrying, because he would stay out all night. With the stress of everything I started having complications with my pregnancy, and had to go on bedrest at about six months. This added even more stress. I was worried about paying the bills. I was then put on bedrest for the remainder of my pregnancy by my doctor. I eventually made the decision, for the health of my unborn child and my mental health, to move back home to Mississippi with Mama and Daddy. Betty Lee was so happy; I think she could have toted my dresser back in the house all by herself.

On June 9, 2000, I gave birth to the most beautiful, curly-haired baby I had ever seen. We named her Quinlyn Kly'desha Sambo. Clyde was not there for the birth because he was on the road driving again, and he did not make it in time. My sisters Shirley and Cynthia were in the labor room with me, and Mama was not far behind coming to the hospital to check on her babies. When I was discharged from the hospital, me and Moonie Pie, as Gloria had nicknamed her because of her big cheeks, went back home with Mama. Clyde went back to Clinton. We still couldn't afford to live together, but I was later able to rent an apartment in Magnolia. Things were still tight; I had gotten a job in MS closer to home, and was living together with my family again. This went smoothly for a few months, until Clyde went to Clinton to hang with his buddies and ended up drinking too much and totaled the only reliable vehicle we had. At this point, I was spiraling down mentally, and I had all I could take. This was the last time we lived together as husband and wife. I moved out of the apartment and went back to Mama house for good, taking my baby with me. Clyde and I continue to talk, and he would come visit Moonie Pie when he was home.

Young people and old people, please stop using these children as a pawn to get back at him for the relationship not working. Stop talking about him to your children, telling them he is not worth nothing, he left us, he left the relationship, not his child. If the father wants to see them, let him see them. I did not hold anything against him, because we started the relationship off wrong. We were unequally yoked. I thought he was my Boaz, but he wasn't, so my Boaz must still be out there. But I will no longer attempt to find him on my own. I will pray and let God send him to me. Even though I suffered mentally during our relationship, I stilled loved him. When I love, I love hard. You can be in love with someone and just not be able to be in a relationship with them. You do not have to leave every relationship bitter. If it does not last, then it wasn't in God's plan for your life. Even though we were technically only married two years, we were biblically married seventeen years because we never divorced. I sent him papers one time and he refused to sign them, even though he was living once again with his oldest daughter's mother. I did not stress it, because I believed in the vows I took "til death do us part." He was now on his own, living in sin, and I was free to just raise my child as best as I could.

After the birth of Quinlyn, and the separation from Clyde, I started to become physically sick. I was going back and forth to the doctor, but they could not find out what was wrong with me. I had lost my appetite, I was aching and in pain, and I always felt horrible. Then to add to all that, Quinlyn had problems when she started to walk. She would walk a short distance, then we would have to pick her up. She couldn't voice what was happening, so we just started carrying her on our hip, even though she wasn't a small baby anymore. I could just see people's facial expression asking, "Why they are walking with this big girl on their hips?" My sisters were a great help. We went around to different churches singing because we were a big portion of the church choir, so we would take turns carrying her. And man could we blow, Winding-Carter Church of God in Christ choir was fierce.

Well, my health continued to get worse, and Quin still would not walk. I did as any good mother would; I put my health on the back burner until I found out what was wrong with my baby. I took her to the children's clinic in McComb, and they referred us to Baston Children Hospital in Jackson, MS. I started to get really scared when the children's clinic couldn't find out what was wrong with her, so they referred us to a specialist. I took her to her appointment in Jackson and they ran tests. My baby was diagnosed with rheumatoid arthritis in both of her knees, and that's why she wouldn't walk. The pain was too much for a two-year-old, and I was in disbelief. We had to go every few months to Baston so they could monitor the progression of the disease and her regime of medication they had to put her on.

The doctors at this point still had not figured out what was wrong with me, but I was more worried about my baby. We were still going around to revival after revival carrying her on our hips. It was our revival season in the area, which lasted from June to November, and we usually had a church to visit at least one a week during this time. I will never forget when we were in revival at my daddy's church in Liberty, MS, Mary's Chapel. They called for prayer, and I went up to the Alter carrying my child. Elder Emmanuel Hackett walked straight to us, laid his hand on my baby's knees, and prayed for her. We had just found out she had this condition and hadn't told many people. And as the Bible says, "not many days hence" we went to the hospital in Jackson for a checkup, and they couldn't find it anymore. She was healed. James 5:6 said the effectual fervent prayer of a righteous man availeth much. Prayer still works. We no longer had to go to Jackson for appointments.

Chapter 5

***

The transitioning of my brother

G rowing up, my baby brother Sharron was spoiled because he was the last child of my mama, and he was a boy after my mama had eight girls in a row. It was my sister Barbara Ann that died as a baby, my brother L.E. Jr., my oldest sister Gloria, Celestine, Shirley, Brenda, Renee (named Betty after Mama,) Gale, myself, Cynthia, and then lastly a boy. Sargent Sharron Andre' (Ronnie) Carter was tall and muscular, and was one of the quietest, gentlest, humble souls you could have ever met. He loved his mama and daddy, and they loved him. He was very protective of his sisters, especially Cynthia. He loved us and we loved him. He loved children, and he had a great relationship with all his nephews and nieces. He was a very hard worker; he worked at Walmart distribution Center and was a soldier in the McComb National guard.

In January of 2001 he died suddenly, and that took a toll on the entire family. We had not lost any close relatives in years, and this was the first break in our family chain. It devastated my parents and the rest of us as well. It was like it was a dream. Mama was in the kitchen cooking something that he liked to eat. He was a picky eater, but we made sure something was cooked that he liked. If we didn't cook, we knew a Whopper from Burger King would suffice. We were all going through our normal evening routine, and he was getting ready to go to drill for the weekend. He was ready to go, but looking back on it, he was procrastinating and acting like he really didn't want to go. He picked up Quin and just held her for a little because he was crazy about her, and then he told us bye. For some reason, I felt compelled to go stare out the window as the car was pulling off. That would be the last time we saw him alive. They called us a couple hours later from the National Guard Armory and told us he had collapsed, and they were rushing him by ambulance to Southwest Hospital. We started calling everyone and started to quickly put on clothes, because we did not know how bad he was.

By the time Cynthia, Mama, Daddy, and myself made it to the hospital, more of the family was standing waiting outside. Gloria was the only one at work that night, so we had to call and tell her. She got so upset one of the nurses, Shirley Bates, drove her all the way back to Mississippi. When they found out we were there, they told us to come back to this little room with no windows, and I knew deep down inside this wasn't good. The doctor walked in and told us he did not make it. We were all crying and screaming; we were in shock, he had just left us. They allowed us to go back there a few at a time to view his body. It was like a dream; he was laying on the bed looking so peaceful, like he was asleep. He even had his little crooked smile on his face, but we were in total disbelief. This couldn't be real. They ordered an autopsy because he was so young and appeared in such good shape.

When the autopsy was completed, it showed a heart defect that he shouldn't have lived as long as he had with. They told us he did not suffer, and that he died instantaneously; his heart just stopped. That was a little comforting to us, knowing he didn't suffer, but that didn't change the fact that he was dead and not coming back. We all grieved his death in different ways. Daddy had a nervous breakdown for a while, Mama withdrew into herself; she stopped cooking, stopped driving, her health started to fail her more, she was unable to attend church like she used to. His siblings were trying to be strong for each other, but we were falling apart inside. I know I was. How were we supposed to make it without him? This did not help me at all, I was already depressed because of a failed marriage, and I was raising a child on my own. I had started getting sick. It was just too much to handle. Seeing Mama so sad and heartbroken, and Daddy just confused and not knowing what to do with himself. We all were somewhat lost at this time. But then I heard Lee Williams and the Spiritual QC album, and I started listening to it and going to church more, and that helped me to cope but pain of the loss was still there.

Things were never the same, but we learned how to move forward. Daddy got better, but Mama was never quite the same. She started smiling and enjoying her family, but it was as if a piece of her heart had gone with Sharron. Rest in peace, little brother, you are loved and truly missed.

Chapter 6

***

The transitioning of my Queen and my husband

How do you deal with the loss of the one who nurtured you in their womb? The one who went through labor pains to give your life. The one that made sure you were fed and kept you clean and dry when you were a baby. The one who walked the floor at night to make sure you were covered up and breathing. The one who felt the same pain you felt. The one who had the most beautiful smile that brightened your day whenever you were sad. How do you cope? How do you live without them? How do you not lose your hope?

Well, I couldn't answer these questions at the time, because I went on a downward spiral. I could not cope, all my hope was gone, and I didn't want to live without my mama. Deep down I blamed myself, because I was not there when I thought she needed me the most. Cynthia and I went on cruises every year with a group of church members and other friends in a group called Claude's Family and Friends. This was our fifth or sixth cruise with the group, and we always had a blast. Except the last cruise, something just didn't click for us. The last cruise we went on was in December of 2015. It started off with my usual preparation; I took Mama to the doctor the week before we left, I made sure they had plenty of medication to last for seven days, I made sure they had food in the house, and I called Renee and let her know I was leaving and to cook enough when she cooked to feed Mama, Daddy, and Quin and keep an eye on them.

We left on this cruise on a Saturday morning. But something did not quite feel right. We returned that following Saturday. Soon as we hit land when we got back, I would call and check on them. I learned then Mama had been sick, but refused to let anyone take her to the doctor. She told me, "I was waiting on you to get back and take me." I told her she should have let Renee or someone else take her. So, when I got home and looked at her, I knew something was seriously wrong, and I ended up taking her to the Emergency room. She was admitted into ICU that night with congestive heart failure, and that started her in-and-out ICU stays until we brought her home for good on February 16, her birthday. This was her last time in the hospital because the doctors said there was nothing else they could do for her, and we brought her home on hospice.

I took care of her as best I could, and she always said I bathed her like she was a newborn baby. She was my baby. My sisters and nieces would take turns staying; we put ourselves on a schedule. Everyone would come visit: her grands, great-grands, and great-great-grands, her brother Levi even came from Texas. Her sisters Lou and Mary called almost every day from Detroit. Her sister-in-law Mae called, and her sons-in-law would visit her regularly. Many people called to check on her daily. My cousins Brenda, Beverly, and Faye came to visit. Her niece and nephew Velma and Owen came by. A lot of people felt like they would have been imposing, so they just called. Many sent up prayers—"timbers" as the old folks called them—for her.

March 7th around 3:30 a.m. I heard Gloria scream, "Lisa, she is gone!" The Lord had taken my mama from her earthly home to her Heavenly reward. I was devastated and in disbelief; my Mama was gone. A piece of me left with her, and I was not the same anymore. I felt my life was over. Who was I going to take care of? This was a very, very sad day for the Carter and Amacker families. She played such a huge part in so many lives, and it left so many people at a loss. She had been reunited with her mama, Rosa Lee Amacker, her dad, Willie Amacker, her brothers who she loved so much, Woodrow, Henry, Matthew, and Sam, her baby girl Barbara Ann, and her baby boy Sharron. I knew she was rejoicing, but the ones she left behind were heartbroken. And I was heading into a dark, dark place that seemed to have no return.

Life does not stop with a loved one's death. Clyde kept in touch with me; we talked like two mature adults who had a child together. He would come see Quin when he could. He never did pay child support for her, but Quin was well taken care of by her grandparents, aunties, and cousins. She did not want for anything. Cynthia had even taken the role as a second mom to her and had her spoiled. Things were getting better; we were coping somewhat and functioning to some extent. We were still grieving Mama's death, but the world did seem a little brighter. Then tragedy struck again: Clyde went into renal failure and had to go on dialysis, and his health began to fail. He lasted for a few years, and then I got the call that he was in the hospital in Baton Rouge, LA. He was on life support, brain dead, and his mother Mary wanted the life support removed. We were still legally married, and even though we hadn't lived as husband and wife in over fifteen years it was still my final decision. I had to make the decision to remove the machines. I talked to his mother, and Quin, my baby, said if there was nothing they could do for her daddy she didn't want him to lay there and suffer. I found somebody to sit with Daddy, and to Baton Rouge we headed.

When we got there, Mary and his sister Cherie had left, because they couldn't take seeing him like that. When we made it to the room, his daughter Jamie was there. I always treated her like she was my own daughter. Quin and myself sat with him and talked to him, even though we knew he couldn't respond. I believed he could hear us. We told him how much we loved him. The doctor then came and spoke with me outside in the hall and explained Clyde's condition, and that he would not have any quality of life because he was completely brain dead. So, with a broken heart I signed the papers to remove the machine because it was his mom and daughter's wishes, and as a nurse, I knew there was no hope.

They weren't very long removing the machine. We sat with him, and in less than two hours we witnessed him taking his final breath. I called his mother Mary and his sisters Cherie and Punkin and let them know. We waited for his body to be released to the funeral home, and then we headed back home. This was March of 2017, one year after my Mom had passed. This spiraled me deeper into my dark place.

Chapter 7

✳✳✳

The Transitioning of My Sister and Daddy

What do you do when you haven't been able to come to terms and cope with the tragedies you have faced in the past, and more tragedies happen? What do you do when you are already in a dark place spiraling out of control and you come face to face with death once again? I will tell you what I did: I crashed, a total mental meltdown. The Bible says in 1 Thessalonians 4:13, "But I will not have you to be ignorant, brethren concerning them which are sleep, that you sorrow not, even at others which has no hope."

Webster's defines hope as a desire for some good, accompanied by a slight belief of obtaining it, or a belief that it is obtainable. Holman's Bible Dictionary defines hope as, "A trustful expectation, particularly with the expectation of fulfillment of God's promises." Biblical hope is an expectation of a favorable outcome for your situation. I had lost all hope.

I know on this journey called life, you will face many trials and tribulations. But we also experience many joyous occasions: the birth of a child, job promotions, graduations, and weddings. But on the other hand, we also face one of the most painful, heartbreaking events, and that is death. Family members dying, friends dying one after another. Some people cope with death well, but I am one of many that has problems coping. I have lost both my maternal and paternal grandparents. I have also lost aunts, uncles, cousins and friends that have impacted me tremendously. But to lose my baby brother Sharron at such a young age was devastating. Then the loss of my mama was an unexplainable experience for me, a life-altering experience. The loss of my husband— yes, he was still my husband even though we had lived apart for over fifteen years. I still honored the vows I took all those years before. I honored those holy vows made before God and man. Wedding vows are not just words spoken, you are making an agreement of commitment to a person, and God is your witness. The vows are until death us do part. I honored my vows; I didn't date or entertain a man in any way, because in the eyes of God and in my heart I was still a married woman. Seeing the man I vowed to love, honor, and obey take his last breath will be something I remember for the rest of my life. It did not stop there; now I faced the loss of my sister.

Celestine Carter White was one of the sweetest souls that ever walked this earth. Cele or Stine, as we affectionately called her, wanted to appear stern on the outside, but she was sweet as sugar on the inside. Stine would do anything to help anyone. She was diagnosed with lupus when she was in her thirties, and even though it hit her hard, she didn't let it stop her. She took care of her husband Wendell and her four children, Trevor, Kim, and her set of twin boys, Branton and Britton. She was one of the hardest workers you would ever want to meet, and she instilled that in her sons. Stine's health began to fail, and she became disabled. But even though she could not work outside the home anymore, she still worked. Now she worked by serving the Lord.

My beautiful sister would not miss church. We both loved to sing, so we sung in our church choir and joined the McComb District Choir. This was a combined choir consisting of members from different churches in our district. The District Choir was directed by an awesome director, Michael Robinson. Stine loved to sing; even though her illness had started affecting her heart and breathing, she never stopped singing. Sometimes she would sing so hard that she would have to go vomit as soon as we stopped singing. But that did not discourage her or stop her. The next time we had to sing she was standing right beside me giving it her all. We sung side by side many wonderful years together. My sister's health continued to fail, and she was in and out of the hospital. Her condition was getting worse. I was losing my sister; she had begun the dying process. She had been in the hospital in Hattiesburg, MS. I was one of the family contacts to talk with her nurse about her condition. She was very, very sick at this point. Stine was seeing and talking to our mama.

She was telling Mama, "Mama, your baby is really sick," and I believe she knew death was quickly approaching.

They discharged her from the hospital, and it was late when they finished her papers. Her daughter Kim, who was her caregiver and had done an amazing job taking care of her mom, called me. She wanted to know if I could go over and get her mom situated when she made it in because it was late, and she couldn't leave her kids. Of course I went, that was my sweet sister and nothing would have stopped me. By the time her husband drove up to their home I was already there sitting. I helped her get in the house; she was so weak and had lost so much weight, just looking at her just tore me to pieces. I stayed strong for her. I got her washed up and dressed for bed and tucked in. I made sure she had her medication, and my brother-in-law went to warm her up some soup. I talked with her a little while and we said our goodnights, not knowing we would soon be saying our goodbyes.

A couple of days later I was laying in bed, which was my place of solace, and my phone rang. It was my sister Gloria telling me to come quick, Stine was sick. I jumped out the bed and into the car and raced to her house. When I walked in, I could tell Gloria had been crying, and by the look on Stine's face I knew this was it. We got her ready and called the ambulance. The ambulance came and loaded her in, and Gloria and I followed quick as possible to the hospital. We called all the family; her boys were working in Hammond, LA.

We all gathered and waited while she was being transported into the ICU. We sat in the waiting room and waited and prayed. Finally, the nurse called and said the doctor wanted to talk to us, so they came and took us to a private room. We all knew what that meant; we had been through the same process with Sharron.

We all were escorted to the room where we sat, waited, and prayed. The doctor finally came in; my sister was still alive, but he let us know there nothing else they could do. We were able to go back and say our final goodbyes. Although I knew what was coming, for it to be voiced out loud tore me apart. My brother-in-law, niece, and nephews were devastated; we all were. As we took turns in groups to say our goodbyes it all seemed like a dream, but the dream was a nightmare. In less than two hours, my sweet sister had transitioned from her earthly home to Heavenly reward. My world was turned upside down again, and on a further downward spiral I went.

I was trying my best to go on, but I didn't know what to do. I'd lost my baby brother, and I'd just lost my mama, husband, sister, and a special Auntie Sonja all in the month of March within a three-year time span. I was totally dumbfounded, and the worst part was death came knocking once again. In September of the same year my sister died, my only living parent, my daddy, transitioned. I spiraled completely to rock bottom. This was the man I shared one half of my genetic makeup with. My Superhero, my daddy, could do anything. The first man I had ever loved. He was the last person I was to care for and my pastor. How was I to go on? I was at a complete loss. I wanted people to stop telling me it would be alright, because in the mental state I was in, I had lost it all. I had nothing to live for. Why was I still here? My daughter had graduated high school, and she was living her own life. I had no reason to wake up every morning. My life had no meaning and was not worth living. I had reached the point where I'd lost all hope and the will to live.

Chapter 8

***

No Hope, and a Mustard seed of Faith

At this point in my life, I was at the complete bottom. I had no will or want to even look up. My family noticed the changes in me, but did not know how to help. I was just lost, wandering in my own wilderness, and there seemed to be no exit. I know my family was praying for me, but I was at the point that I could not pray for myself. Intercessory prayer is so important for this reason.

What is intercessory prayer? Intercessory prayer is going to God in prayer on someone else's behalf. Sometimes you lose the will to even pray for yourself. I'm a living witness that can attest to this and its hell on earth when you've lost the will to pray and have lost all hope.

Major depression had set in, and I was in the darkest place of my entire life. I feel my life is over and the only thing left for me was death and it could not come quick enough. My life had spiraled completely out of control, and I could not understand why this was happening to me. I was a believer, I was saved and filled with the precious Holy Ghost, I was the director of the church choir, the junior church Mother, I loved the Lord, and I was in church every time the door opened. Why me? The catalyst in my life began. Time had passed, and we were heading into the worst time in our national history; a virus called COVID-19 had affected the entire world. Now the coronavirus had been here for years, but this strain, COVID-19, is a new deadly strain. This strain has caused the death of so many people, and was so devastating it even shut down the nation. All this happened at a time when I couldn't cope with death already, and to hear about hundreds of thousands of people dying, I went into total mental meltdown.

January 2020 was the beginning of my hell here on earth. I got so bad mentally that even though I was in a depressed state, I didn't want to be alone. I would just pace my house all day from room to room. I was at a complete loss. I started waking up at around eight o'clock every morning, and I would go to my sister Gloria's house and stay over there all day until she left for work in Baton Rouge at about four-thirty in the evening. She would drop me off at my house on her way out. I would unlock my front door and lock it back, turn off my lights, and crawl in the bed for the rest of the night. I didn't fix dinner or anything; if I was hungry, I just went to bed hungry. I didn't have the mind or will to cook, or even put food in the microwave. I hadn't cooked or turned on the stove in over a year, despite how much I loved to cook big meals and feed as many as I could. I had lost the will to do it.

This was my daily routine until COVID-19 got really bad, and we were ordered to shelter in place by the government. This was in March of 2020, so I started staying at my house alone, even Quin was gone. My sister Gale had gone to Kansas with her daughter Brittany and her four kids. Gale called me in March and told me to tell Quin they were hiring mental health techs at the hospital she was working at, and the pay was really good. I told Quin and she decided to go. I was happy she was going, because I knew the shape she was seeing me in was taking a toll on her. I would be in the house with my child I gave birth to, and could not have a conversation with her. She would call me when she would go to work or out and about to see if I had eaten. I could not talk to my own baby, all we did was text each other even when we were in the house together. She left and headed to Kansas, and I was relieved she was gone, because I was tired of her seeing me in the shape I was in.

Since COVID-19 was so bad and we were ordered to stay home, I started a different daily routine. I would wake up the same time around eight; my body had set its own time clock. I would get up and go in the living room. I would get on the reclining chair or the sofa and watch tv until about five in evening. Then I would get in the bed for the rest of the night and begin my routine again the next day. I had received a prayer towel from Pastor Dywon Lewis in the mail that I would lay in the bed with me while I slept. I knew then I had a little faith left in me. But I just wanted to die. The only way I would have food or even eat was when my sister Gloria cooked and would send me a plate by my niece Rondrea (affectionately nicknamed after my baby brother as Ronni,) my goddaughter Mckayln, or my nephew KJ so I could eat. I hadn't been to the grocery store or any store in over a year. I had not been to the doctor in over a year. I had not taken medication in over a year, even though I had plenty of medication and just couldn't find the energy or will to even opened the bottle and take them (this included Lupus medications, high blood pressure medications, and depression medication, among others.) My niece Brandi would drop me off food if she cooked. My nephew Kendrick's wife Tara would drop me off snacks and cleaning supplies. The only way I got groceries is when I would send for snacks by my sister Renee or whoever was going to the store. My sister Cynthia would get off work at the hospital in Baton Rouge and go to Sam's before she would come home and buy enough groceries for both of us. Her food bill would be over four hundred dollars every time she went. She would drop me off microwave food (because she knew I wasn't going to cook) and sodas and snacks for me to eat. My great nieces and nephews: Amaria (who always affectionately called me Nana when she was little and still does, she told me it was short for banana) Sweet Baby, Snooty Bug, Riley, Bud, and Biggie would always come check on me, because they knew I was alone. Thank God for family, or I would have starved to death.

Death was everywhere by this time; all you heard was this person or that person died. Actors and Actresses were dying left and right. Church of God in Christ Bishops were dying of COVID-19 at an alarming rate. In April of 2020, death came to someone dear to our family, James Williams of the Electrifying Crown Seekers of Marrero, LA. The Electrifying Crown Seekers were a renowned gospel group. His death hit me hard, because he was the first person dear to me that had passed since COVID-19 had gotten out of control. James was an amazing song writer, singer, and a phenomenal guitar player. He could make that guitar talk. I had known him all my life. James, his wife Lynn, and the group worked with our church choir for a program we had every year. His death really impacted me, and I was already in a dark place.

In April, I lost my Uncle Ernest Carter, my daddy's last brother. How much more could one person handle? I know they say God will not put more on you than you can bear. I did not believe that though, not in the mental state I was in. My life went on like this until July of 2020, when Cynthia had enough and brought me to her house. I packed a few items, and she came and picked me up to go home with her. I do not know why I went, because I still believed I would not do any better there. I was just wasting her time. There was no hope for me.

Chapter 9

***

A Sister's Love

"Sister, you are like my angel that always glows, you are one of the greatest gifts my heart will ever know." Unknown author.

After Cynthia took me to her house to stay, nothing had changed. I had just changed beds. I was now laying in the bed at her house every day. From the bed to the couch, she still had to make me eat, and I still wasn't taking any medication. This went on about a week or two, then she said, "Lisa, (my nickname) you are going to Dr. Anazia." I told her I would go tomorrow, but when tomorrow came I put it off for another day. I was not planning on going anytime soon.

About a week later she had enough. She came in the room and said, "Lisa, get up and get dressed, you're going to the doctor." I got up, but I was so mad with her that in my head I was screaming. I knew not to voice it out loud, but if she could have only read my mind, oh boy. So, we went to Dr Anazia's office that day. Cynthia went back with me to the exam room, and it's a good thing she did, because I couldn't tell the doctor what was going on with me. She had to go in there and tell the doctor what was going on, because I couldn't even get my words together to voice what was wrong. After we left the doctor's office, we stopped to pick up my medication and went back to my sister's house, and I crawled right back into bed. I started taking my medication for a few days like prescribed, then I slipped back into my old routine and stopped. Cynthia asked me a few days later, "Are you taking your medicine?" I knew I had stopped, and she would be mad, so I lied. I told her yeah, I was taking it. A few more days passed, and she asked me again, and I thought about lying to her again, but with the look of worry and concern on her face I just couldn't. I told her the truth, that I had stoped taking them. She was so upset with me she said, "Give me your medicine, I'm going to give it to you every day." She looked at me with such a hurt facial expression and asked me, "Why just tell me why you stopped taking it?" I just looked at her and shook my head; I couldn't answer her, because I didn't have an answer myself.

Cynthia said, "Give me your medicine, I'm going to give it to you from now on." She got my medicine, fixed my morning dose, and watched me take it. Then she said, "Open your mouth so I can make sure you swallowed it." I used to do this with some of my noncompliant patients when I was practicing nursing, and her hurtful look made something snap inside of me. I told her, "Cynt, you don't have to do that. I'm going to take my medicine. I promise, just give me one chance." At first she said no, but I kept pleading with her and she agreed. From that moment on, I took my medicine twice a day as ordered, every day.

But that's all that had changed; I was taking my medication, but I was still in the bed all day or laying around on the sofa. This went on for another week or so, then Cynt told me she was rushing every day trying to fix her lunch to take with her, and she needed me to start helping her fix her lunch. I just looked at her because I didn't want to do it, as much as I loved cooking for my family in the past. I just didn't think I could do it. I could not remember how to season my food. But I didn't want to disappoint her, so I said ok. I would not use the stove, so I used the air fryer. Begrudgingly, I started fixing her lunch. I did not want to do it, but I forced myself to do it and it was a struggle.

I continued to fix her lunch, but I still wasn't any better. I would fix her lunch and make sure she had everything she needed together before she left. But when she left at about five o'clock every day for work, as soon as I heard her truck start up and her backing out I would turn off all the lights, set the alarm, and get in the bed for the night. This became my daily routine. One time Cynt even came back because she had forgotten something. I knew I had gotten caught, but she didn't say anything that night or the next day, so I felt like I had gotten away with it. I just kept doing it every day. If I had fixed enough food when I made her lunch, I would eat. If I had not, I would just go to bed hungry. I still didn't care whether I lived or died.

This went on until November. Then I encountered death once again. My Aunt Doll, my daddy's sister, called to let us know Uncle Charlie had died. Uncle Charlie was the husband of Aunt Gladys, my daddy's other sister. This hit me hard, I was tired of my family dying. I was in such a dark place I couldn't even call and talk to her. I didn't know what to say. I let her and my cousins down when they needed support, and that is something I would have to live with.

Towards the end of November, something had really snapped in me. It was as if I had totally melted down mentally. I became paranoid that people were out to get me. I kept looking out the window. When someone would knock on the door, I would jump out of my skin. I could not sleep at night because I thought someone would come in the house. I was setting the alarm every night, and would constantly check and make sure it was still armed. Cynt saw something was going on that was really bad and told me, "You are going back to Dr Anazia." I stalled her as long as I could.

Thanksgiving came and I did not cook anything. My sister Shirley cooked, and we went over to her house to get a plate. I could not wait to get that plate and get home, back behind the locked door and the alarm and feel safe. I could feel Cynt watching my behavior, but it was nothing I could do;

I was too scared to hide behind the mask that I was living behind.

A couple weeks later we were in the month of December, and Cynt had had enough once again, and told me, "You are going back to Dr Anazia. We are going to have to put you somewhere to get some help, you not getting better you getting worse." It was planned that I would go to the doctor the next day, and go into Freedom Behavior Hospital in Magnolia. I was about to be committed to a mental hospital. But we received a call from my sister Brenda early the next morning, her baby boy, my nephew Donovan, had been killed in a car wreck in Louisiana. I was faced with death once again. Why me?

Here I was again, deep in more grief. Here I was, trying to comfort my sister, in the worst place mentally of my entire life. Nothing seemed real. My reality had left me. I was convinced that Donnie, as we affectionately called him, was not dead, this was just a trick somebody was playing on us. In a couple weeks Donnie would come back and everything would be fine.

I kept my appointment at Dr Anazia, but I told them I couldn't go into Freedom right now. I wanted to be with my family during this time. It was agreed that I would be admitted the next Monday after the funeral on Sunday. We went to help Brenda make funeral arrangements, but I wasn't much help, because I couldn't even think straight at this time. Cynthia was helping Brenda with the arrangements, and I was just watching because deep down I believed this wasn't real. It seemed like a dream, but my dream soon became a nightmare. I just could not grip the concept that he was dead. Even when we went to the funeral home to view the body before the services the next day, I still didn't believe it was real. Even when I walked in the chapel and saw the casket from a distance, I thought to myself, "It's going to be empty." When I walked up with my sister Brenda and she was devastated, and I looked down into his face, I still didn't believe it was real. The next day at the funeral, I still did not believe it was real. I believed that Donnie would show up in a few weeks, and this was only somebody playing a trick. My family told me later that I had this strange look on my face that day; it was because I had lost touch with reality.

A few of us met at my house in the country after the services. I was walking around in a daze. I thought people had put cameras in my house and were watching me, that they were recording our conversations. I could not wait until everyone was ready to go and I could lock up my house, get to Cynt's house, lock the door, and set the alarm. All the way home I felt like somebody was following us. The next day I refused to go to the doctor to get my paperwork for admission, and I guess Cynt was not in the mood to make me go, so I settled back into my normal daily routine.

Christmas came and I did not cook. I did not buy the kids any gifts because I wasn't going to the store and didn't have the mind to do any shopping online. Cynt and I went to the country to Gloria's house to get Christmas dinner, but I didn't want to stay long, so we got our plates to go and left. Once again, I felt all the way home somebody was watching us. I couldn't wait to get in the house to set the alarm, where I felt safe.

Chapter 10

***

When God flips the switch

We are now headed into the new year 2021. The year of 2020 had been the worst year in US history, and in my life. But things are about to change. About two days before New Year's Day, Cynt told me we were going to cook for New Year's Day. I told her that I had not cooked a big meal in years, and I couldn't remember how to do it. She was adamant we are cooking. So, we went to get the ingredients we needed for the meal. Cynt told me "Lisa, we are not going into twenty-twenty-one like we were in twenty-twenty."

January 1, 2021, a miracle happened! It was like God woke me up and flipped a switch. I got up and got dressed. I went in the kitchen and cooked a full course meal. I cooked black-eyed peas and rice, cabbages, mac and cheese homemade, barbecue ribs and chicken, and cornbread. We ate good that day. I started to cook big meals: mustard greens, mac and cheese, yams (I can't remember ever cooking yams before,) barbecue chicken, and corn bread. I cooked so much I took my Pastor Micah Carter, my niece Tip, and the kids dinner. I started cooking big pots of chicken noodle soup. I hadn't made soup in over four and a half years, since my

Mama died; it was one of her favorite meals that I cooked. The Lord is still working miracles. Prayer still works.

At the end of January, Gloria decided to take a staffing assignment in Kansas, at the hospital Gale is working. She asked me if I would come with her to watch her great-grandbaby Riley that she is keeping right now, while her mom Rodrionna is working in Colorado. I thought about it for a while, and decided to go, since the change of scenery may do me good. I thought maybe the change in the scenery would further help my healing, and it did.

I had been in Kansas about two days when the Lord woke me up at about three a.m. and started bringing things to my remembrance. He let me know I had been in this state since my mama died almost five years earlier, and it was time for me to come out. He let me know the enemy meant that last mental meltdown to be the end for me. But God said not so.

I had lost all interest in church. We had six a.m. prayer on Saturday mornings, prayer meeting six o'clock on Wednesday night, and Sunday School on Sunday morning by conference call since the pandemic had started. I started off calling every conference call saying my name to be announced to other callers, then I started calling but not saying my name, and finally I stopped calling at all. As much as I love gospel music (I'm the choir director,) I started hating the sound of it. When Cynt would play her worship music I would say to myself, "I wish she would turn that off." I would even go in the other room and turn on the TV to cover up the music. I would not even pick up my Bible to read or even pray for myself. And I kept asking myself, "Why me?" I'd been raised in the church and been in the church all my life, my daddy was my Pastor, now my nephew is my Pastor, my mama was a sanctified lady, I'm saved and sanctified since I was young.

I am 52 years old now, I'm active in church, I'm the Junior Church Mother, I'm the choir director, I'm head of the kitchen committee, I was the former youth department director until I stepped down when I became the caregiver for my Mom, and most importantly I love the Lord. I kept asking, "Why me Lord?" I have dedicated my whole life to you. But the question I needed to ask was, "Why *not* me?"

Why did I think I was exempt from the trials and tribulations that the Bible says we are going to face? Why did I think just because I am saved that I was exempt from the heartache and pain of losing my loved ones? What made me so special to God (who is not a respecter of persons) that he would treat me differently?

As saints of God, when we are active in the church and hold a title and life gets too hard for us to handle, for appearance's sake we start to hide behind a mask. We use the mask to cover up our shortcomings from our family, our church family and friends. We hide what we are going through behind a façade, to not be frowned on by people. We worry about being talked about by people. We worry about being talked about like Job was talked about by his friends. "What has she done to be going through all this? Surely, she has done something wrong." But I'm standing on Job's words "Though you slay me, yet will I trust God!" Satan is not the only one that slays you; people talking about you and what you are going through can slay you just as bad.

This is why I wanted to write my testimony. The Lord told me to share it, and if I can't speak it, then write it down. This is part of my healing process. We must realize that Jesus can heal us instantaneously, because he is just that powerful. But sometimes our healing comes in a process. There are some things we have to go back and address, there are people we have hurt we must go back and apologize to, and there are people who are going through the same things we are going through, and he has compelled us to reach out and help them. Our motto should be like the military: "No one left behind."

As Jesus uttered on the cross when he spoke his final words, "It is finished!"

Made in the USA
Middletown, DE
09 January 2023